LETTER TRACING FOR KIDS

KINSLEY

TRACE MY NAME WORKBOOK

Can't Find Your Name?

Have our elves create a personalized book with the name of your choice today!

VISIT US AT:
PERSONALIZETHISBOOK.COM

Chiquita publishing

ABOUT ME

MY NAME IS:

Kinsley

I LIVE IN:

I AM ☐ YEARS OLD.

For parents

For kids

DRAW YOU AND YOUR FAMILY

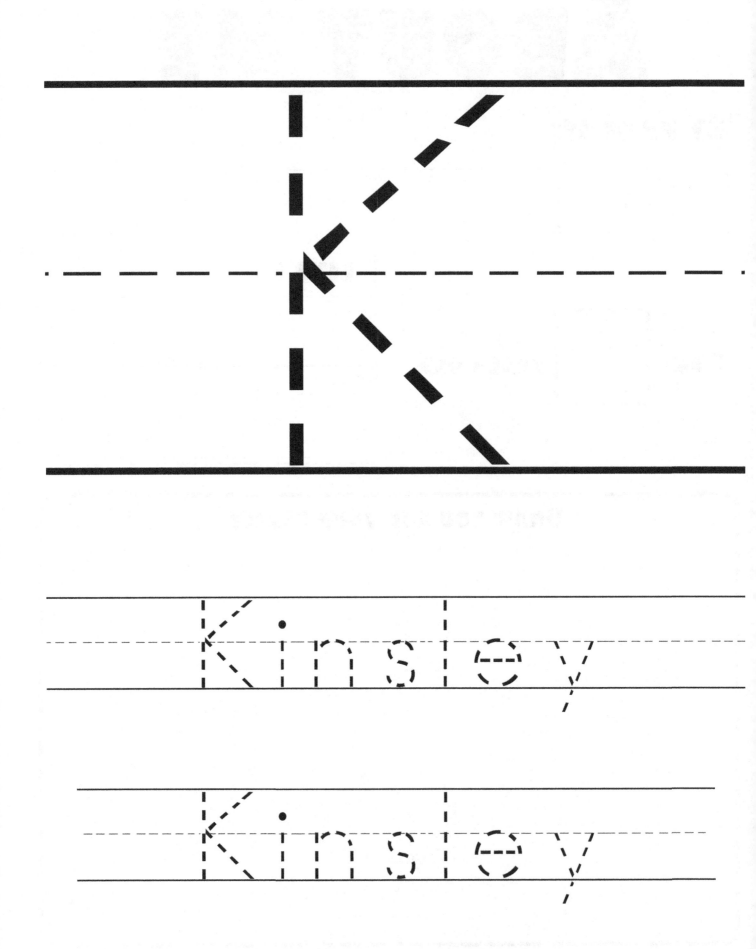

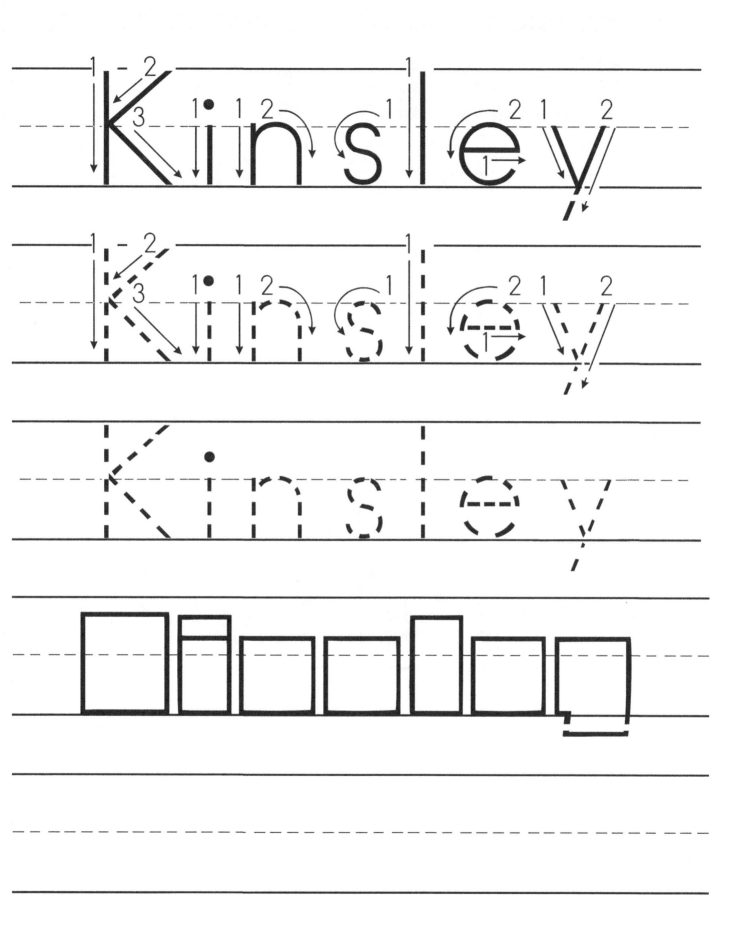

THIS IS HOW I WRITE MY NAME

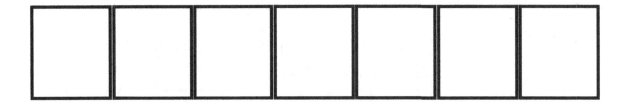

MY NAME HAS ___ LETTERS

1	2	3	4	5	6	7	8

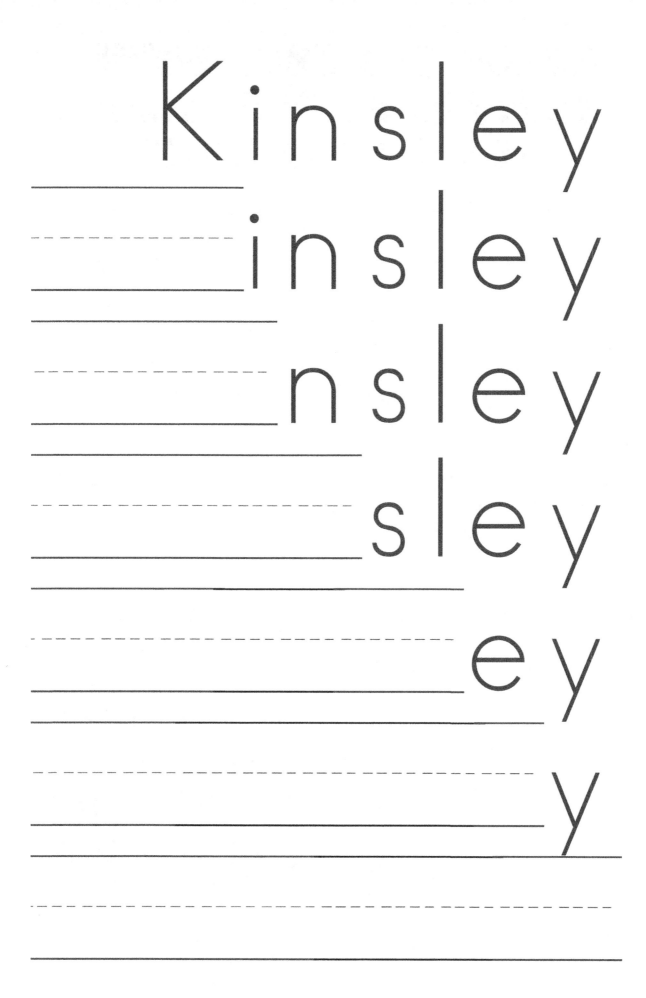

COLOR THE EGGS WITH LETTERS OF OUR NAME WRITE YOUR NAME

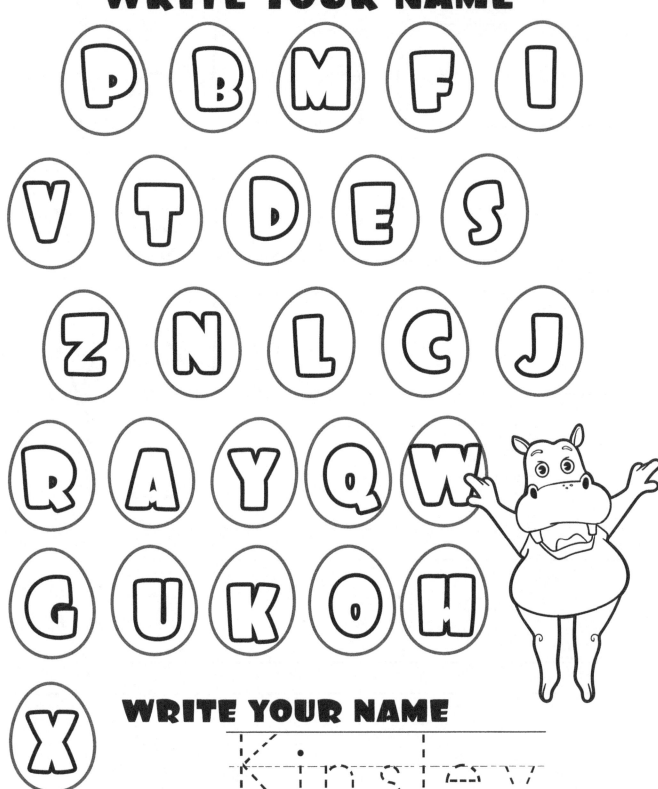

P B M F I

V T D E S

Z N L C J

R A Y Q W

G U K O H

X

WRITE YOUR NAME

Kinsley

WRITE YOU NAME WITH,

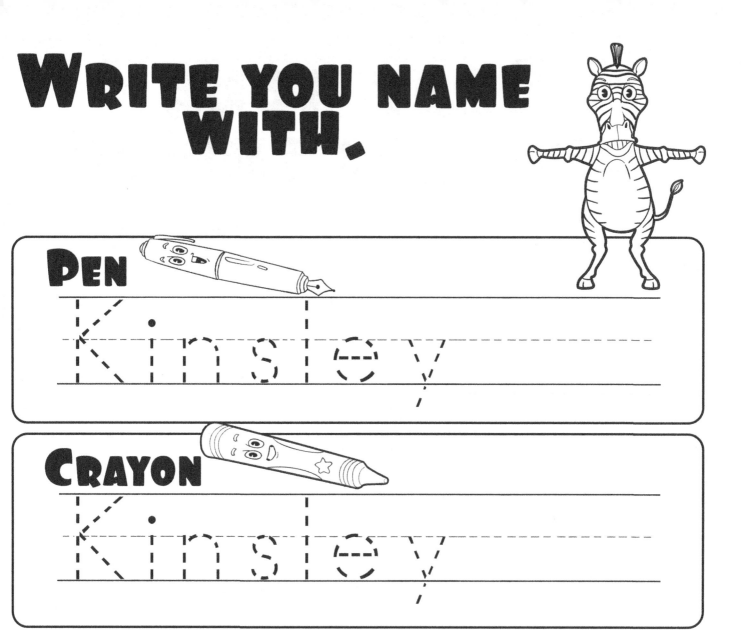

PEN

Kinsley

CRAYON

Kinsley

WRITE YOUR NAME IN BLUE

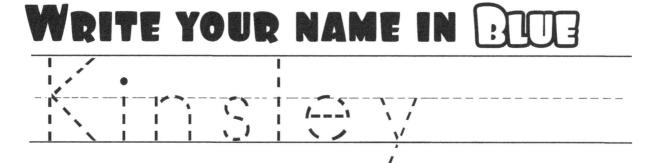

Kinsley

WRITE YOUR NAME IN YELLOW

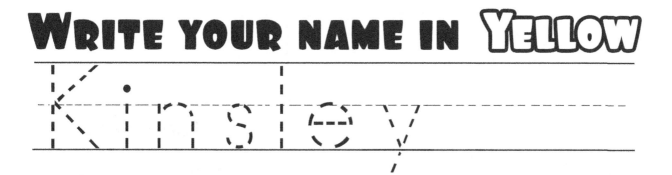

Kinsley

DRAW YOUR FAVORITE THINGS

COLOR

FOOD

TOY

ANIMAL

MY NAME

My name starts with	My name ends with
_____	_____

FILL THE LETTERS OF YOUR NAME WHITH DIFFERENT COLORS

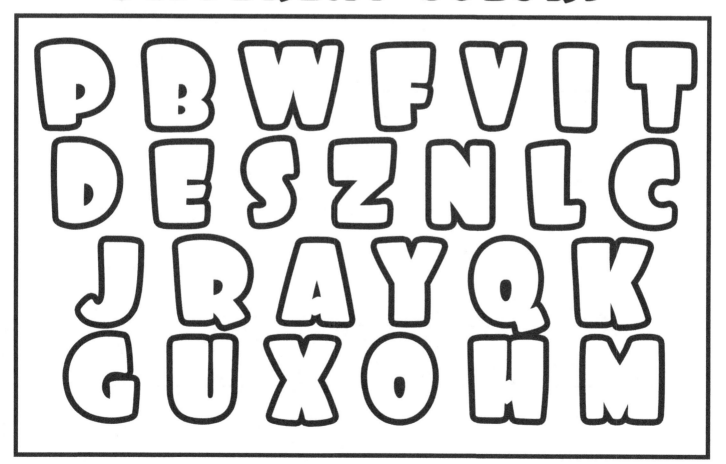

P B W F V I T
D E S Z N L C
J R A Y Q K
G U X O H M

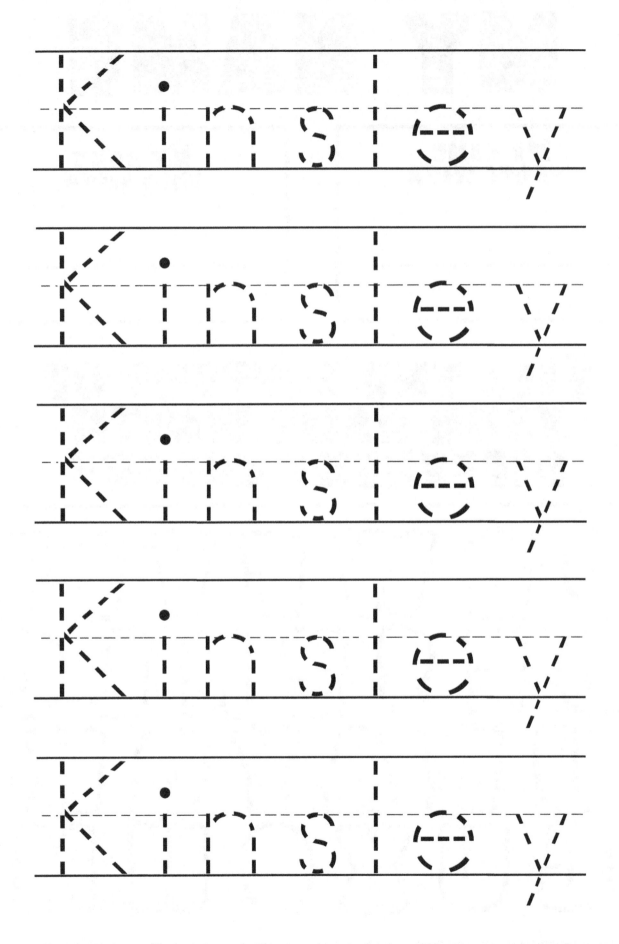

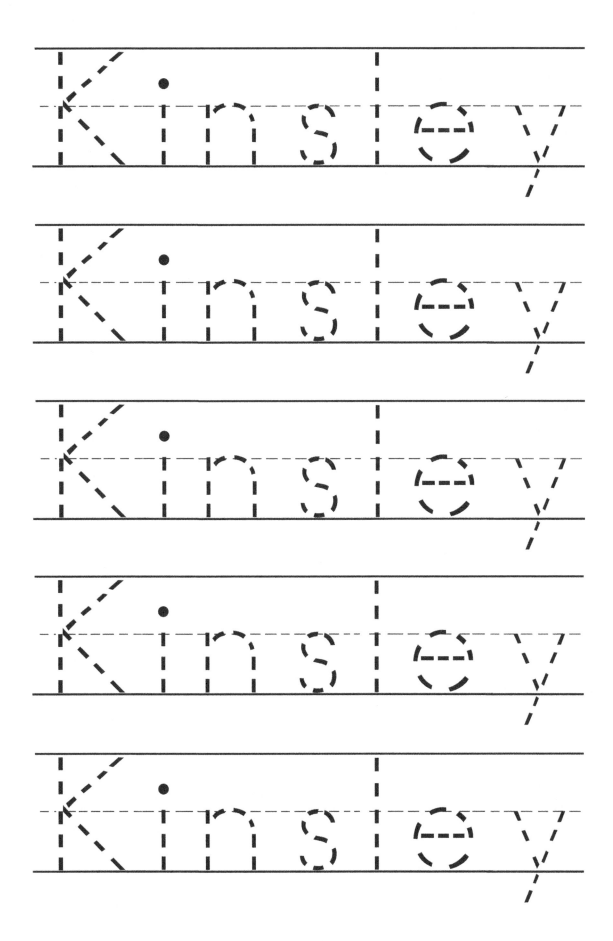

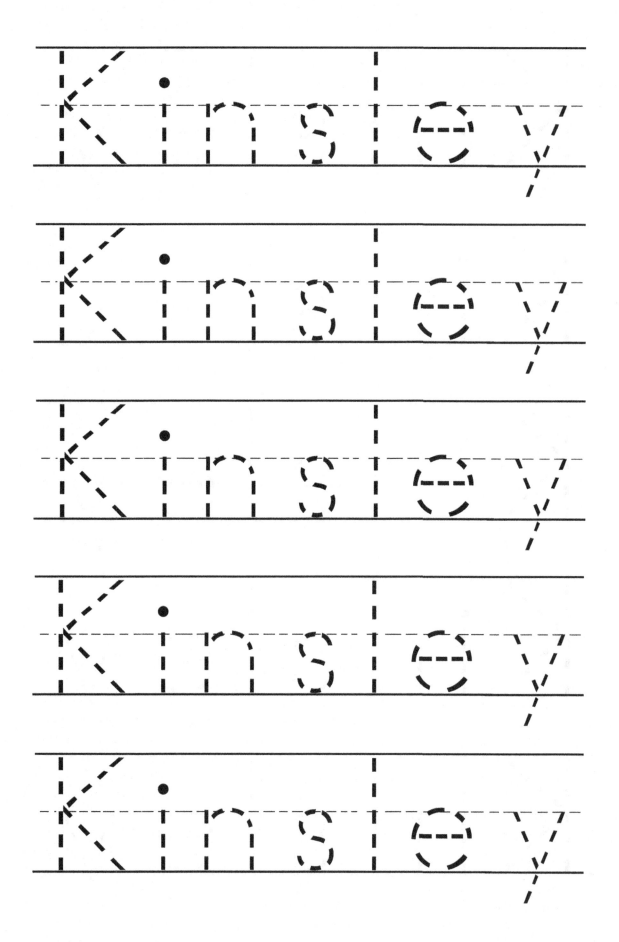

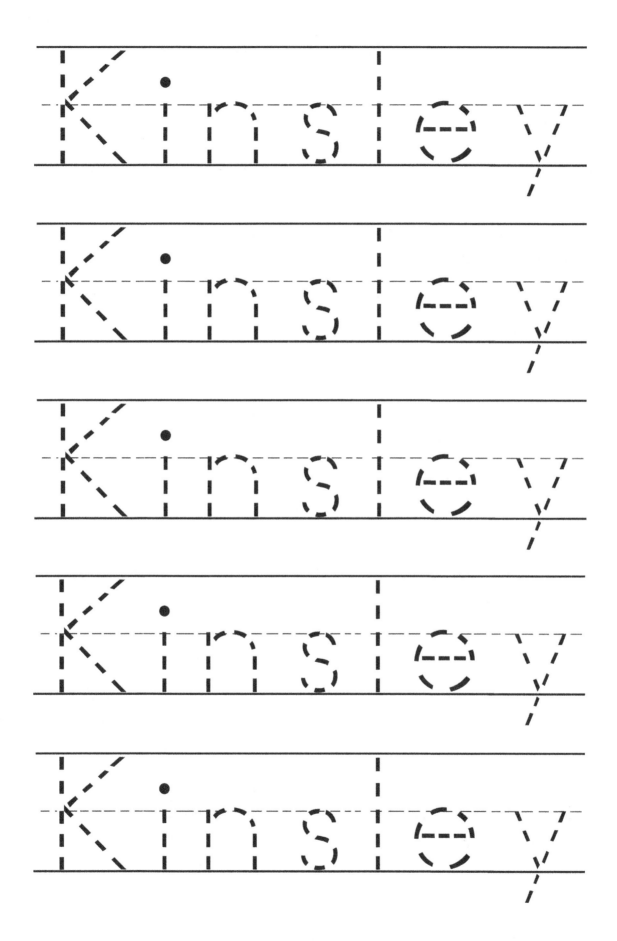

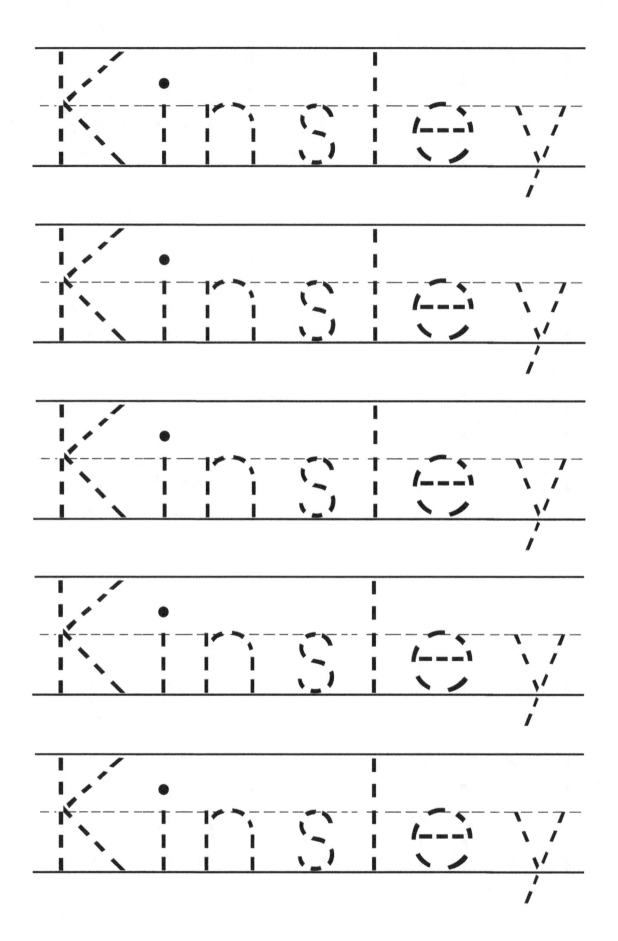

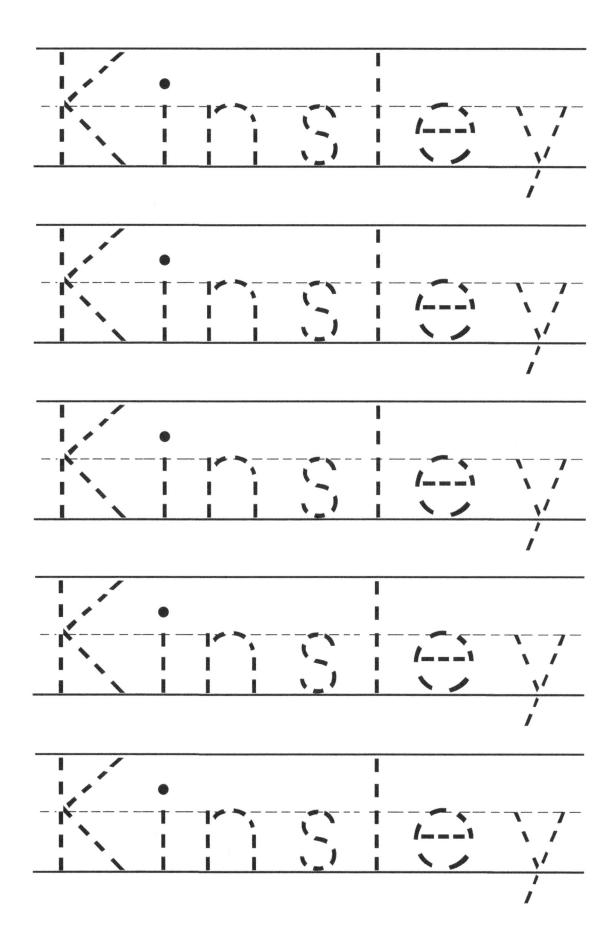

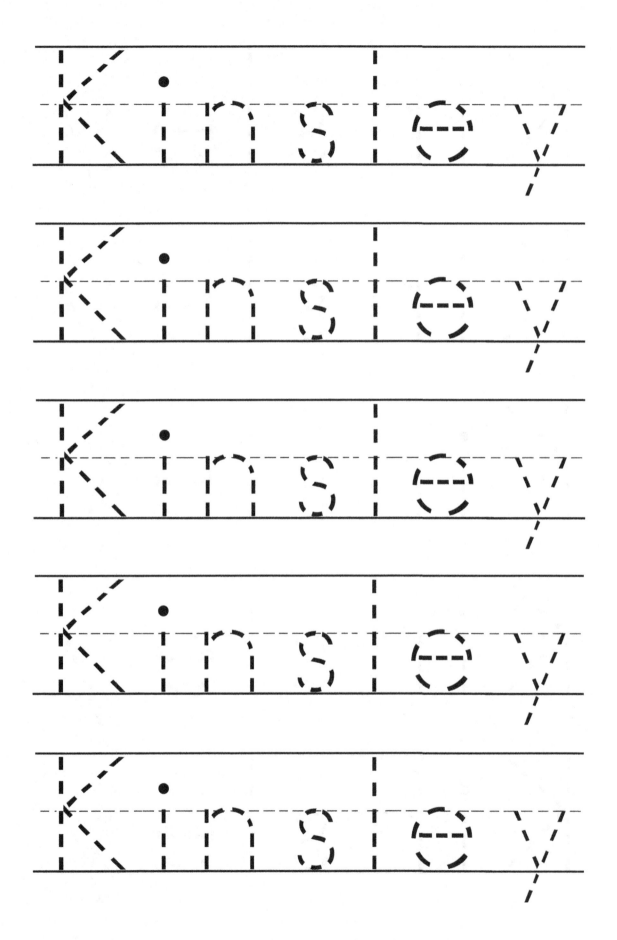

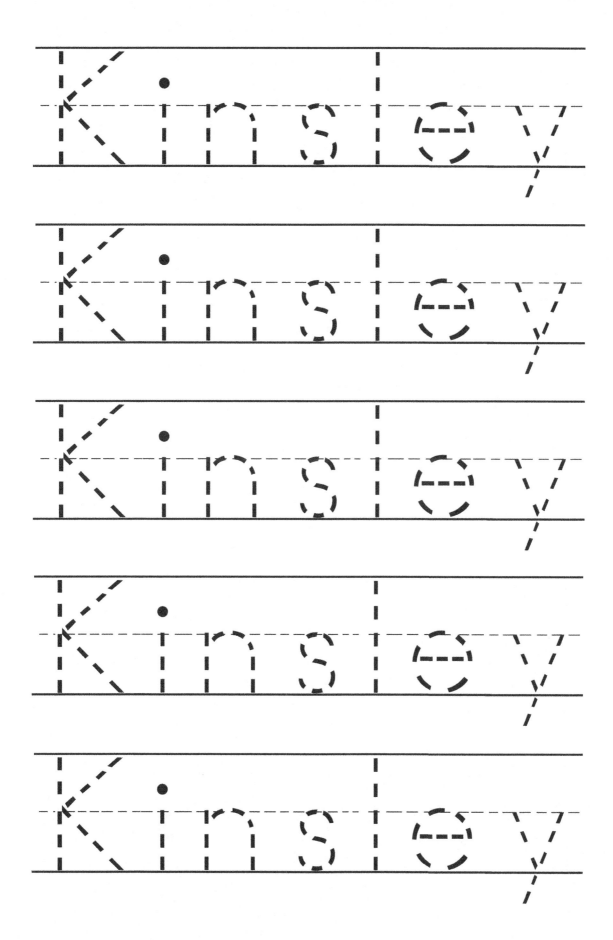

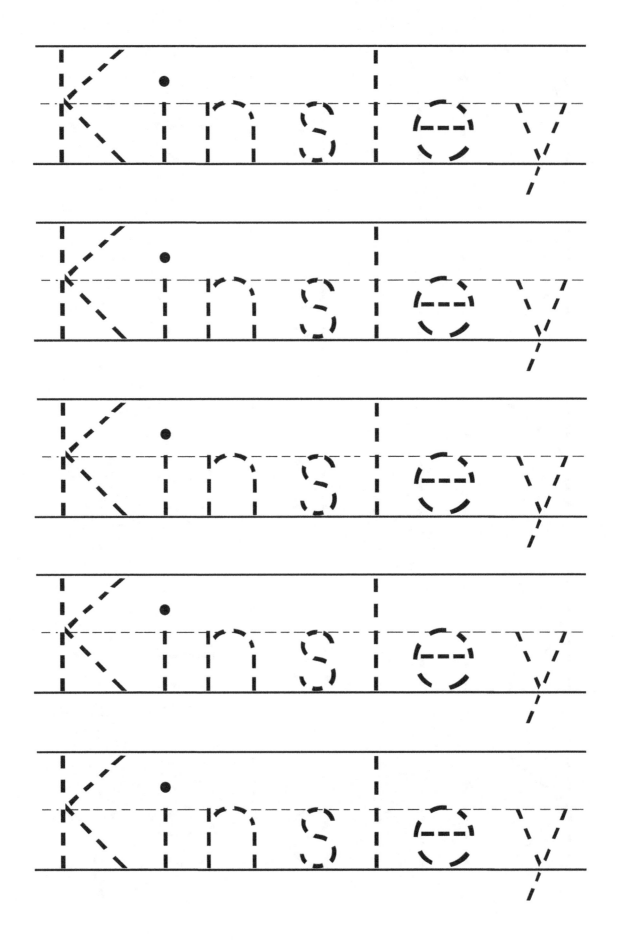

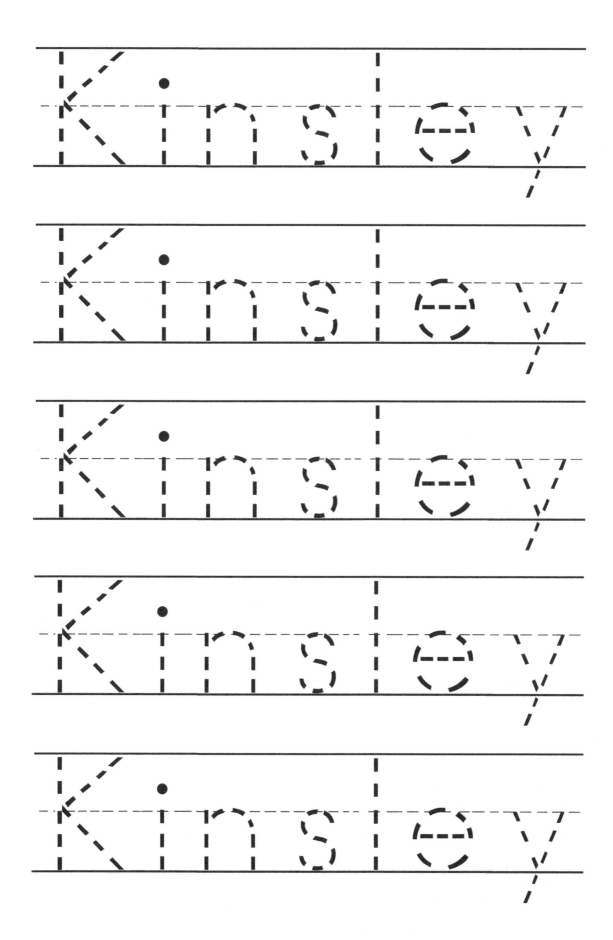

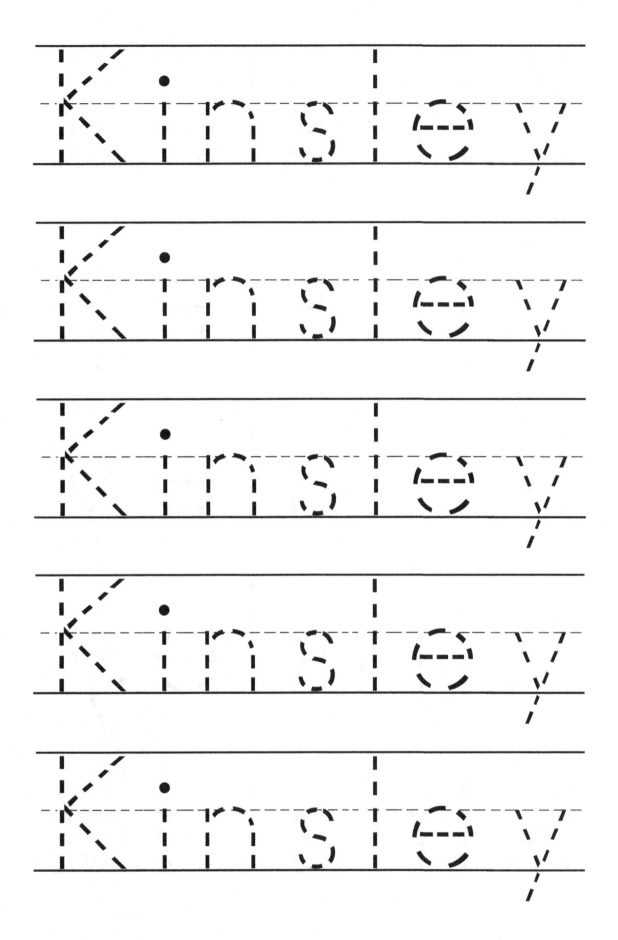

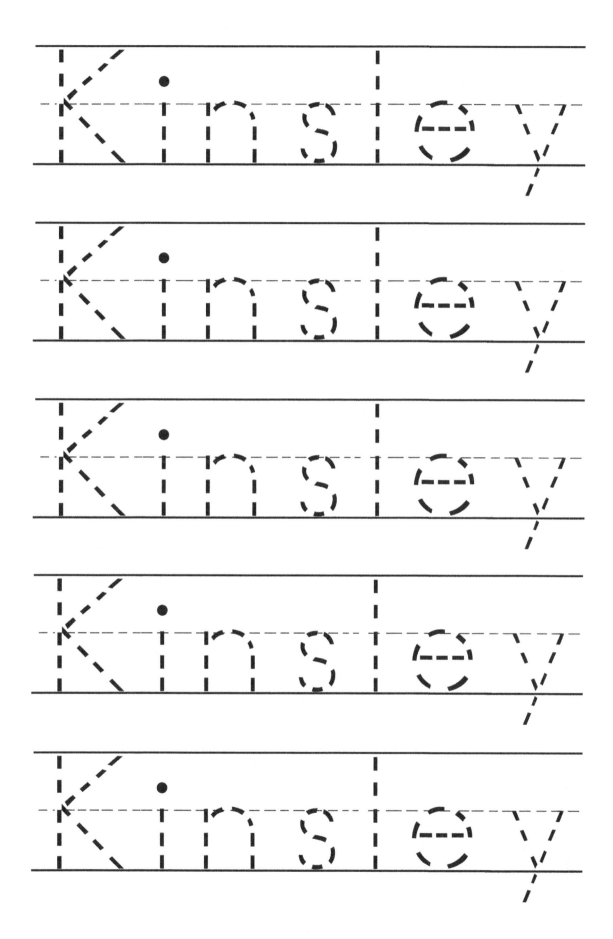

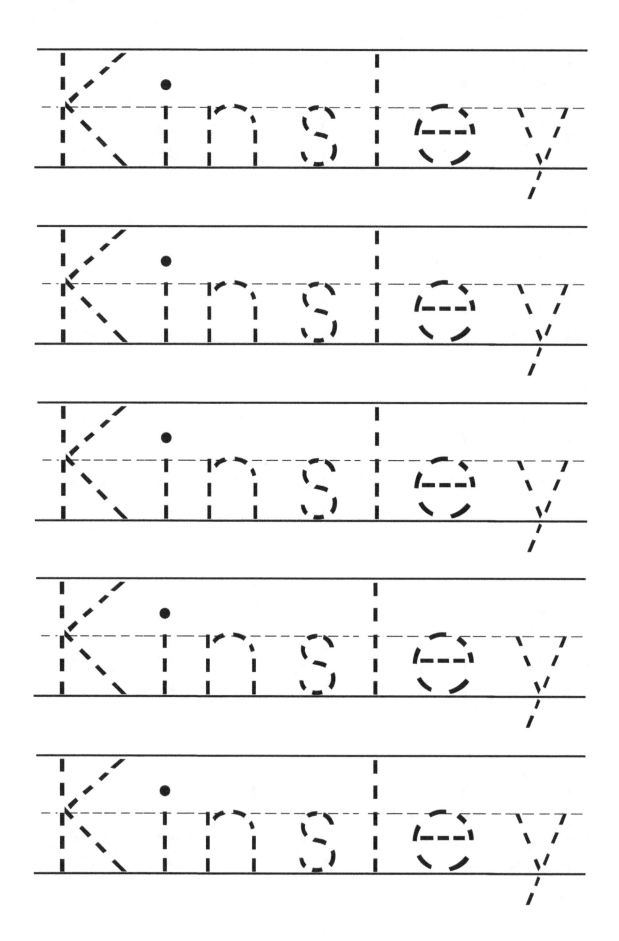

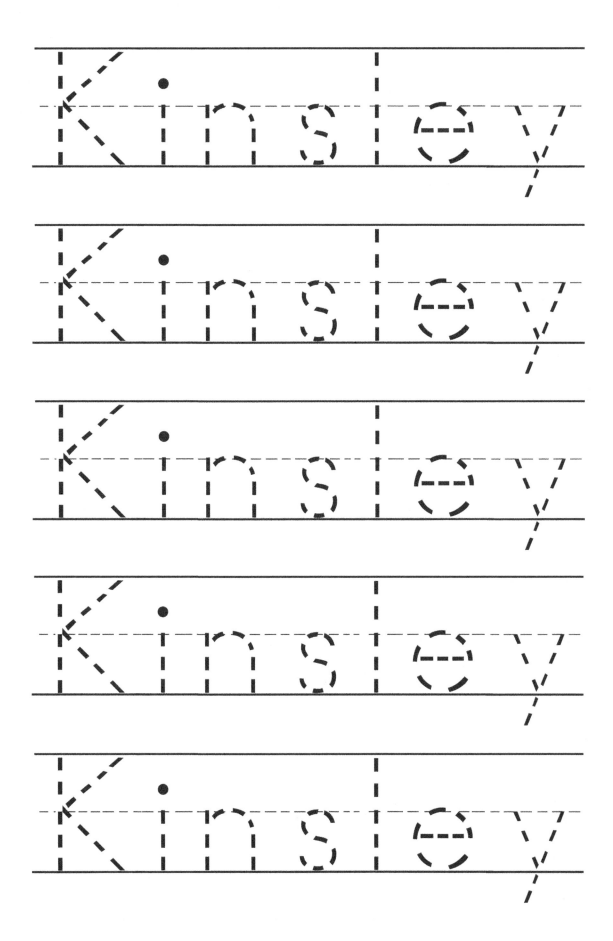

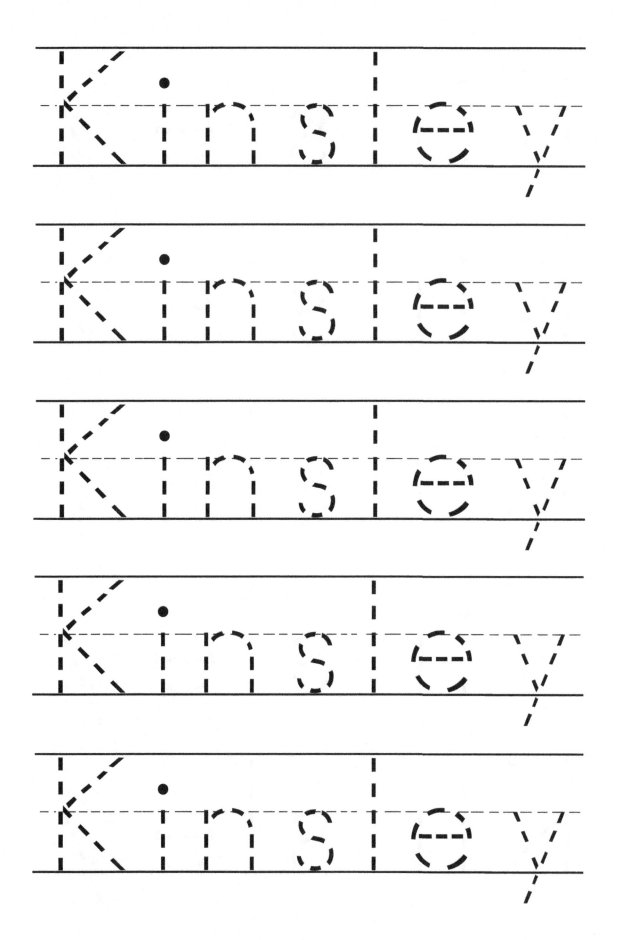

K K K K

K K K K

K K K K

K K K K

K K K K

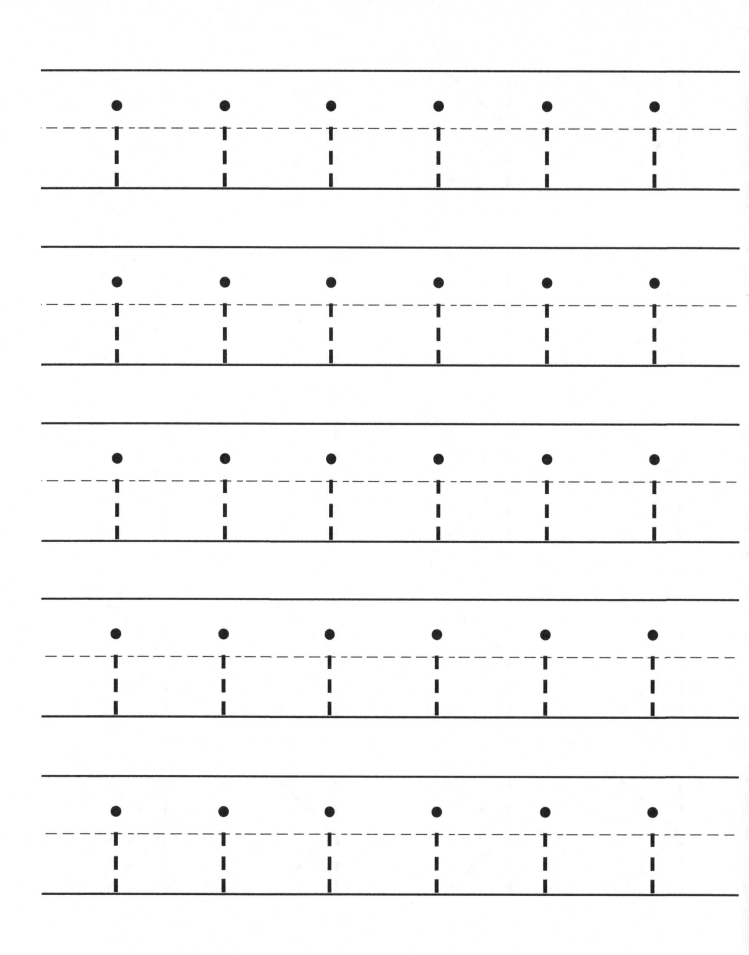

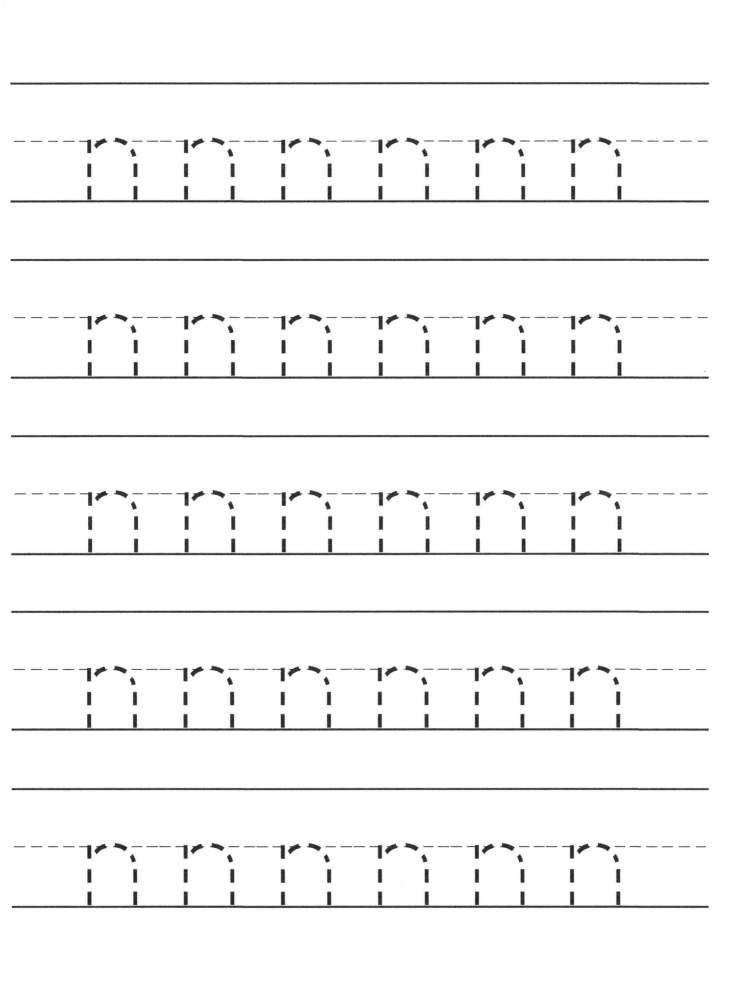

S   S   S   S   S

S   S   S   S   S

S   S   S   S   S

S   S   S   S   S

S   S   S   S   S

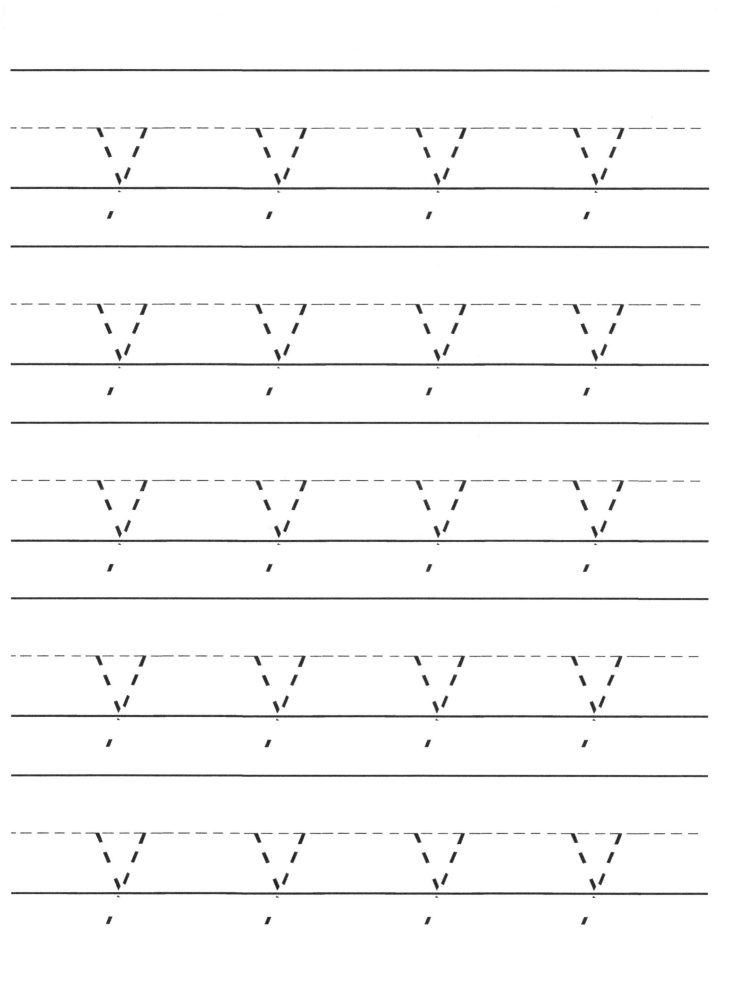

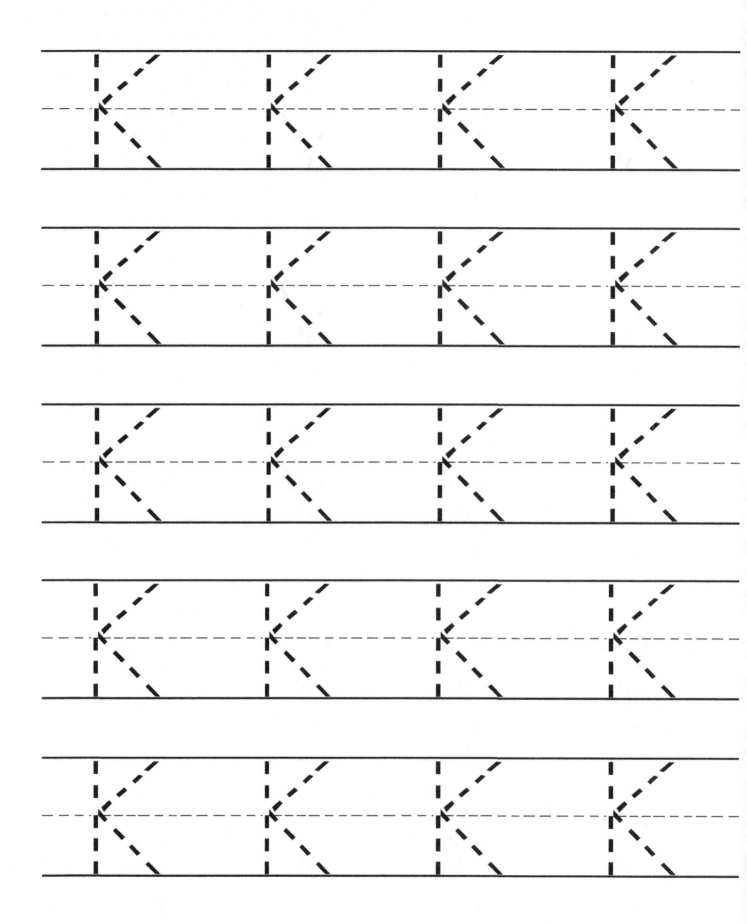

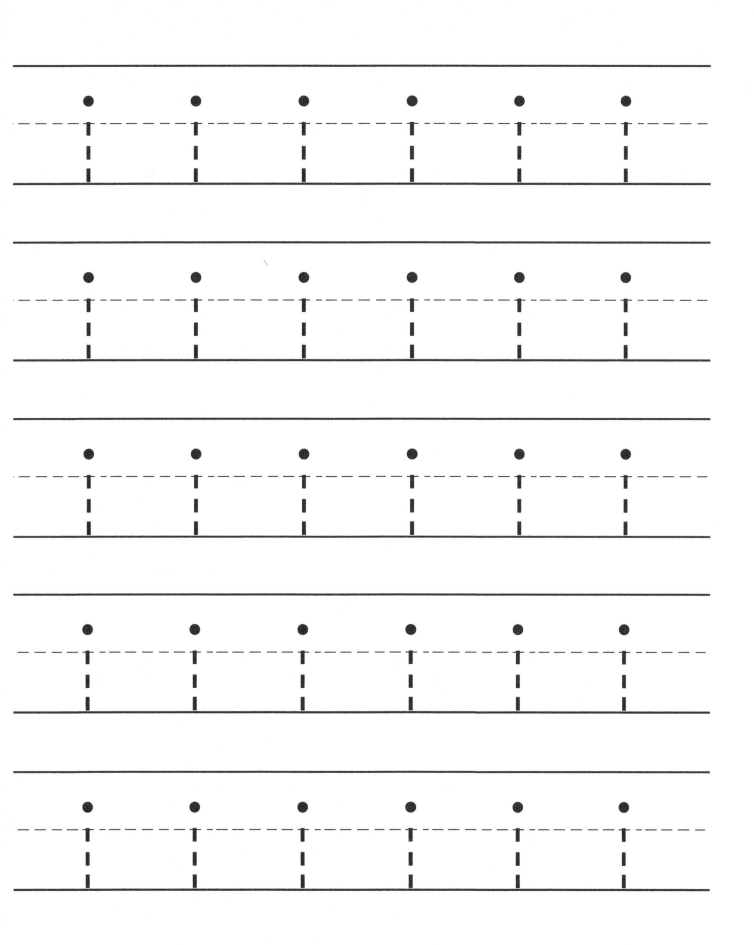

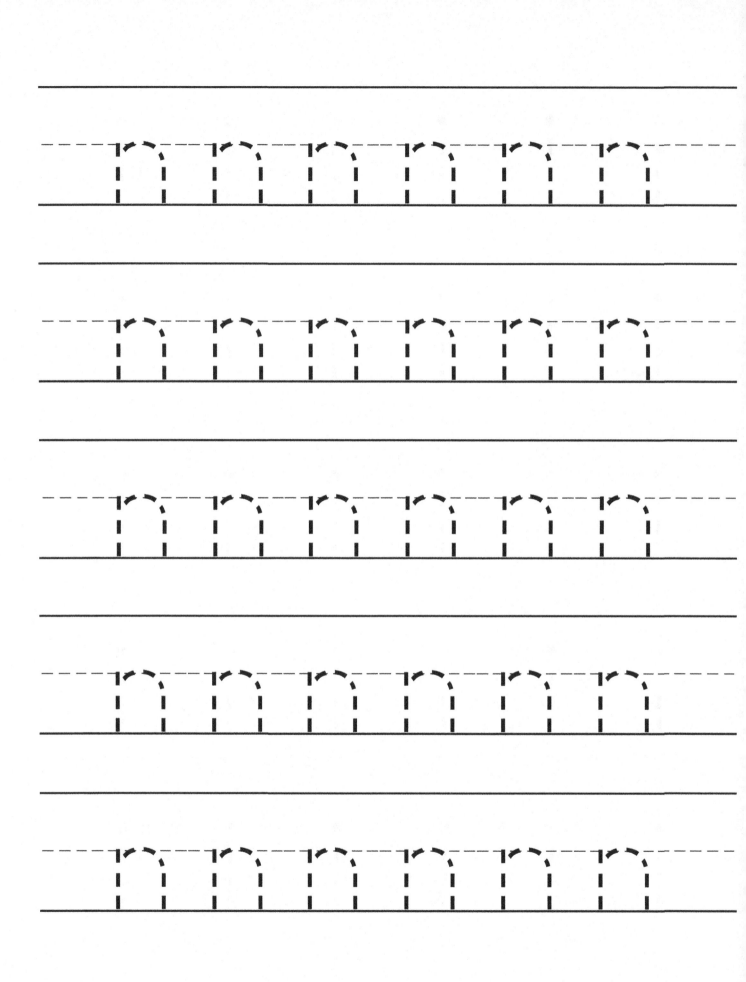

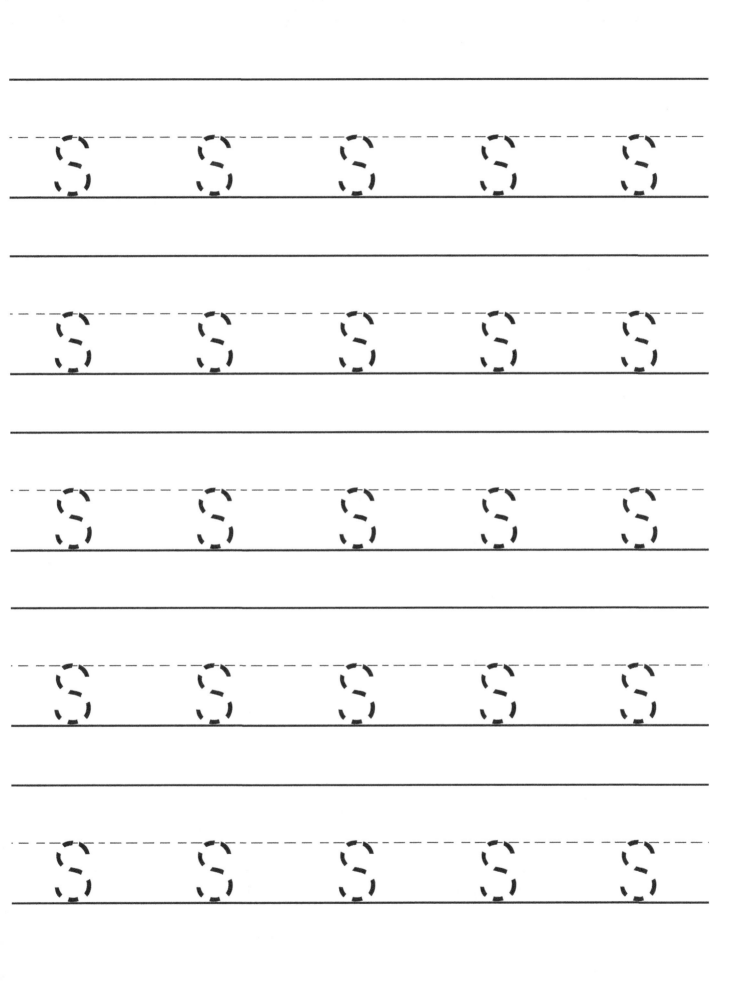

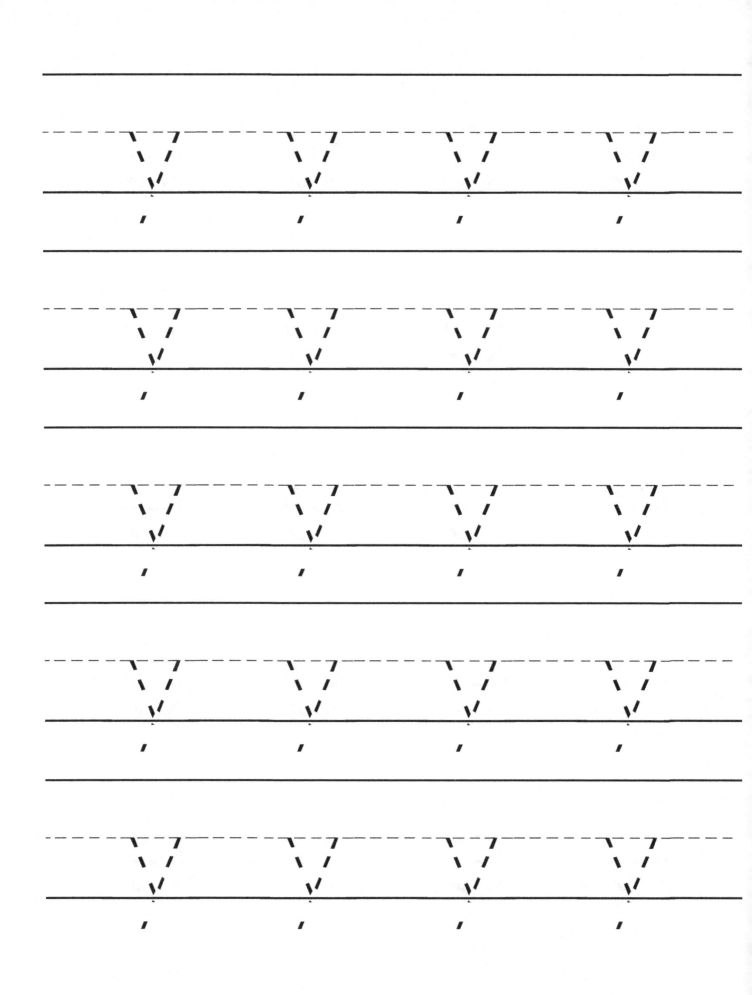

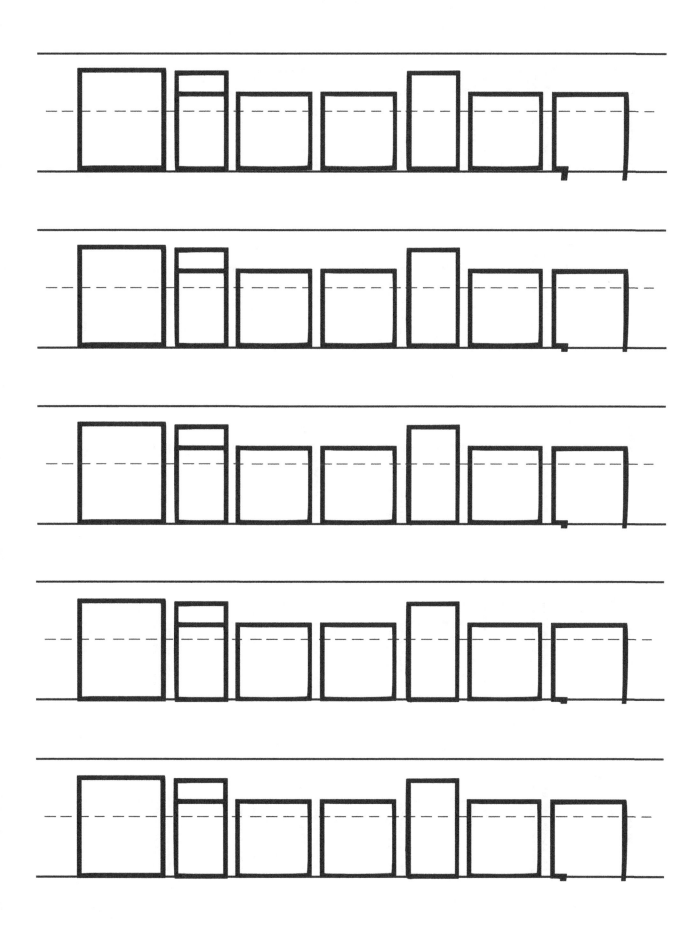

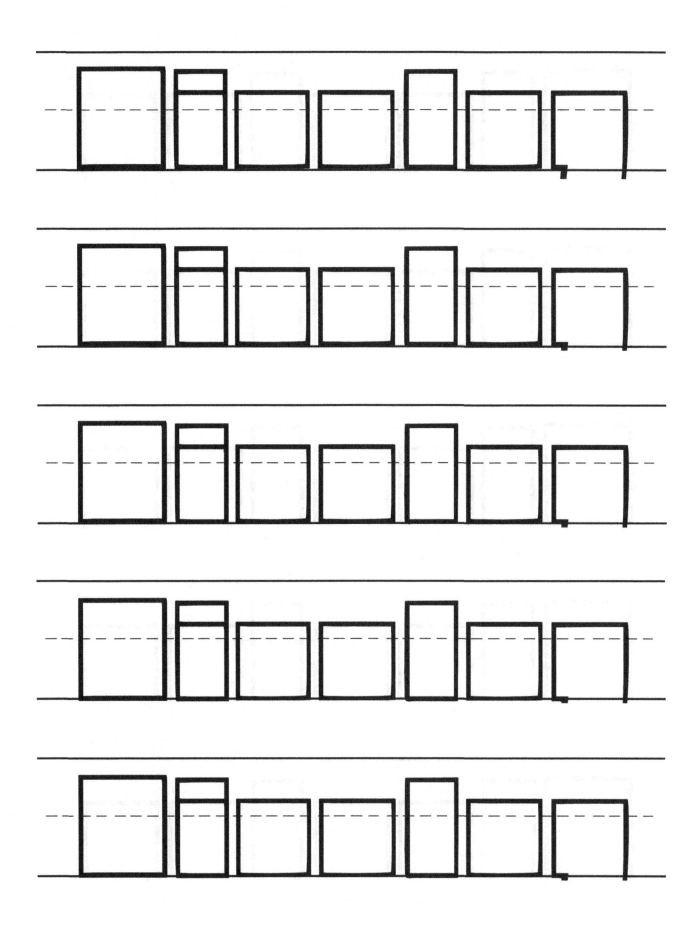

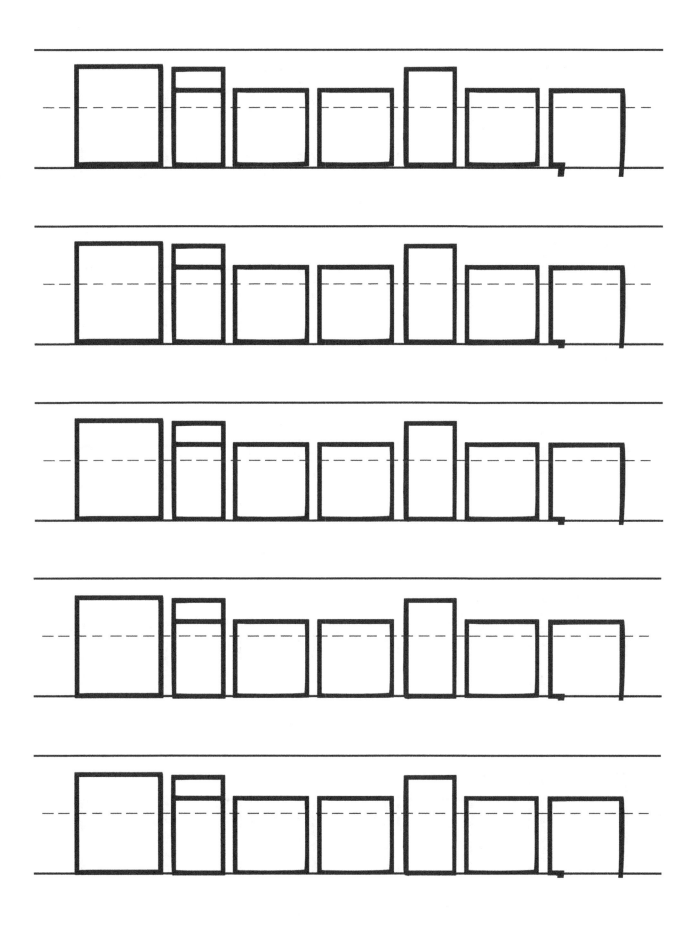

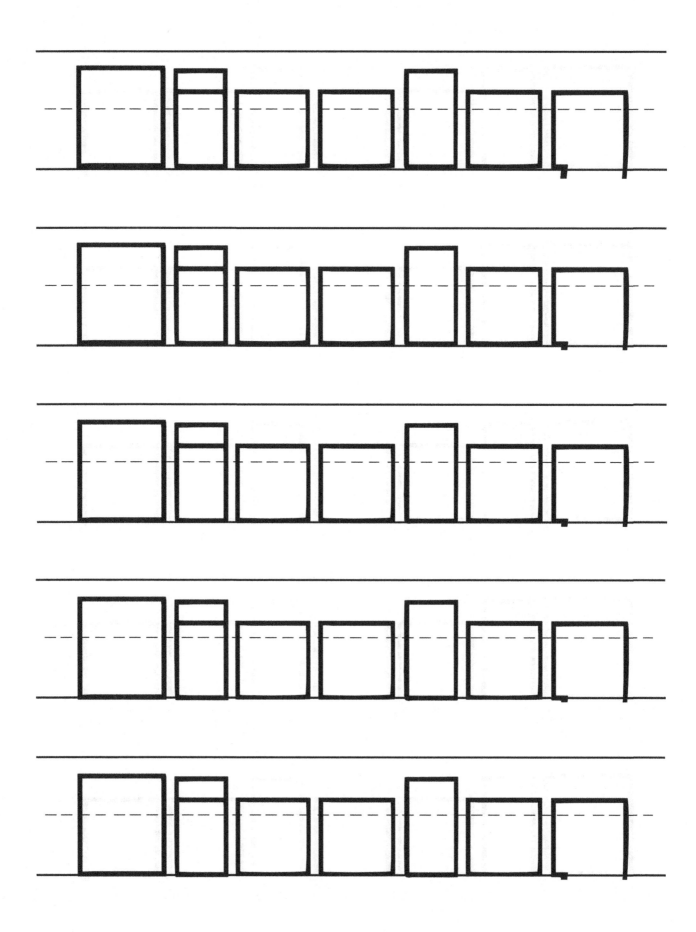

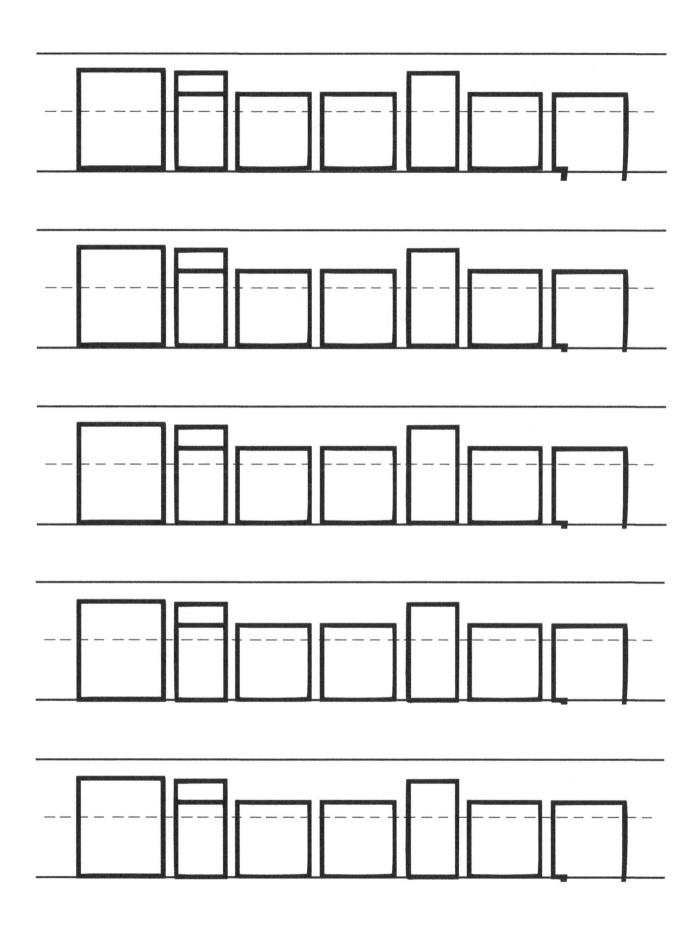

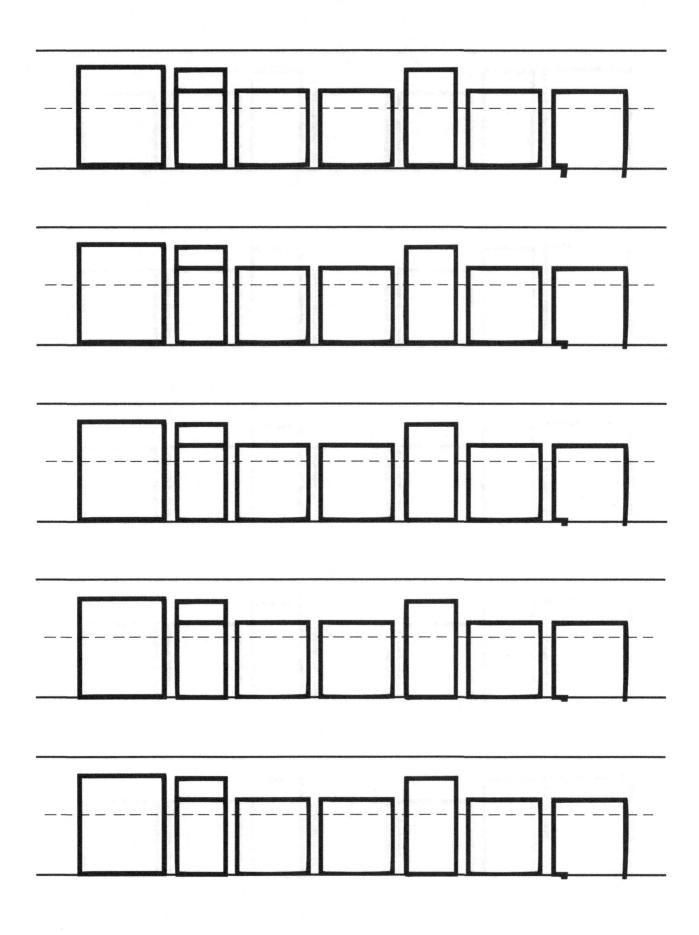

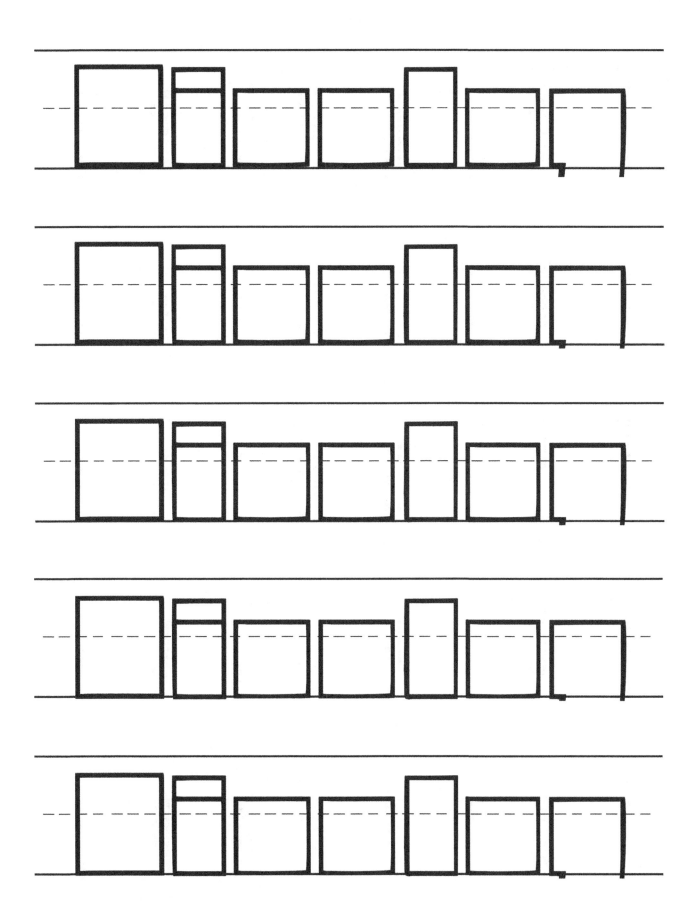

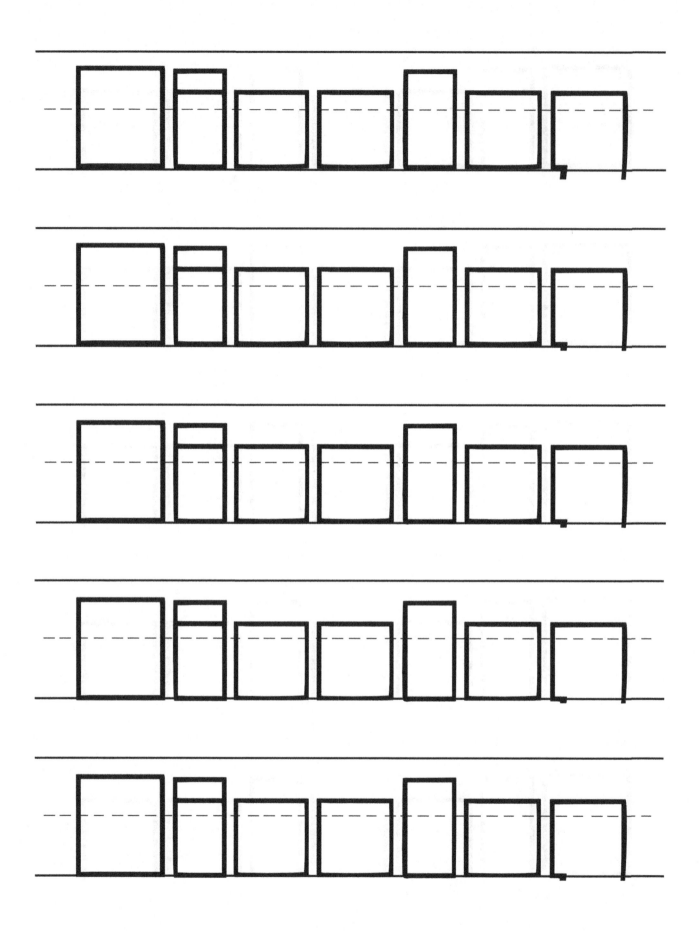

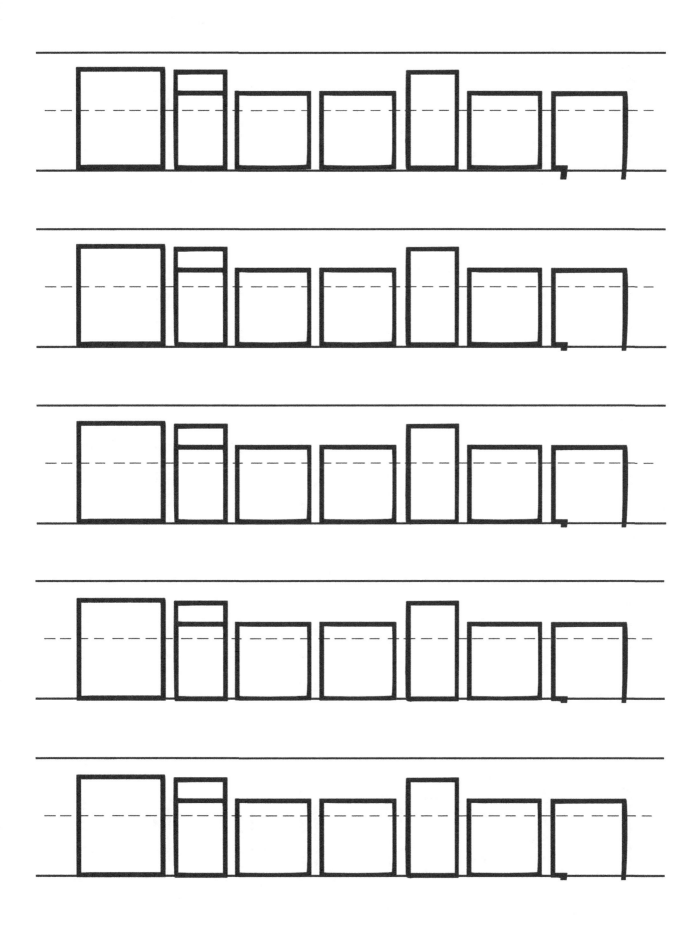

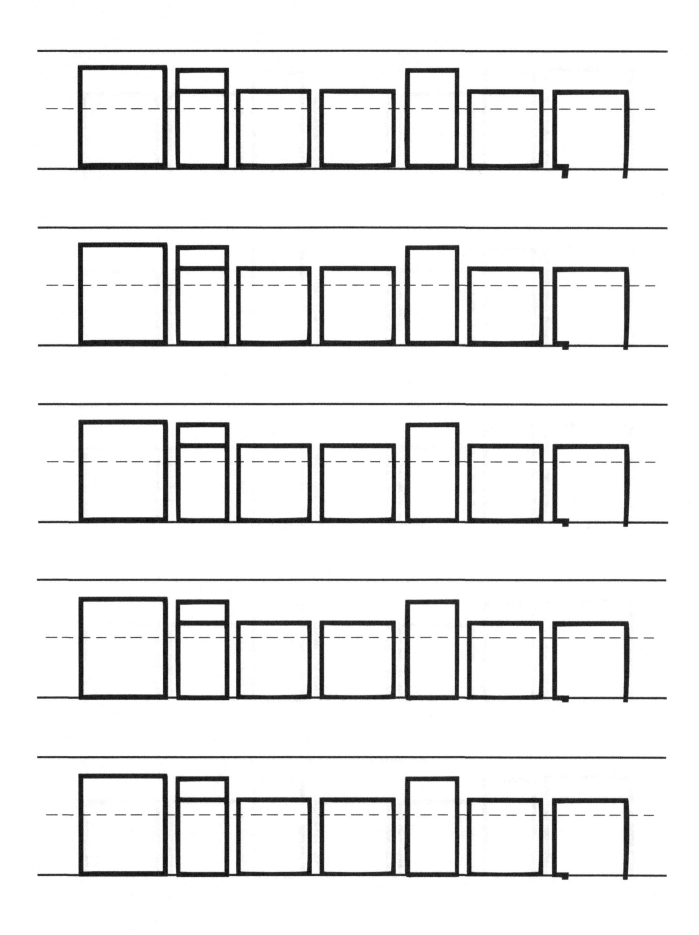

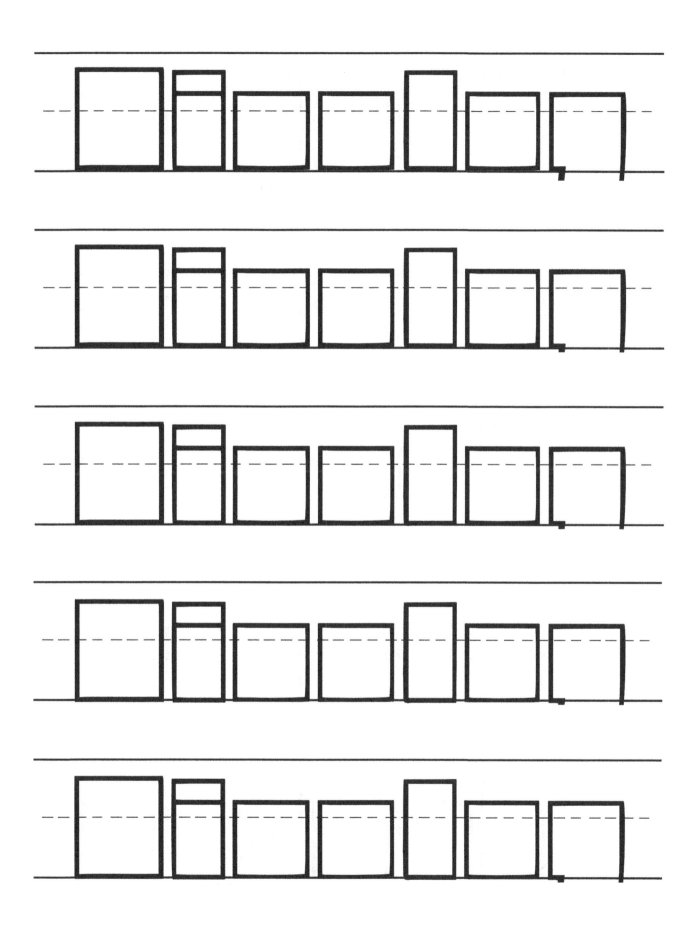

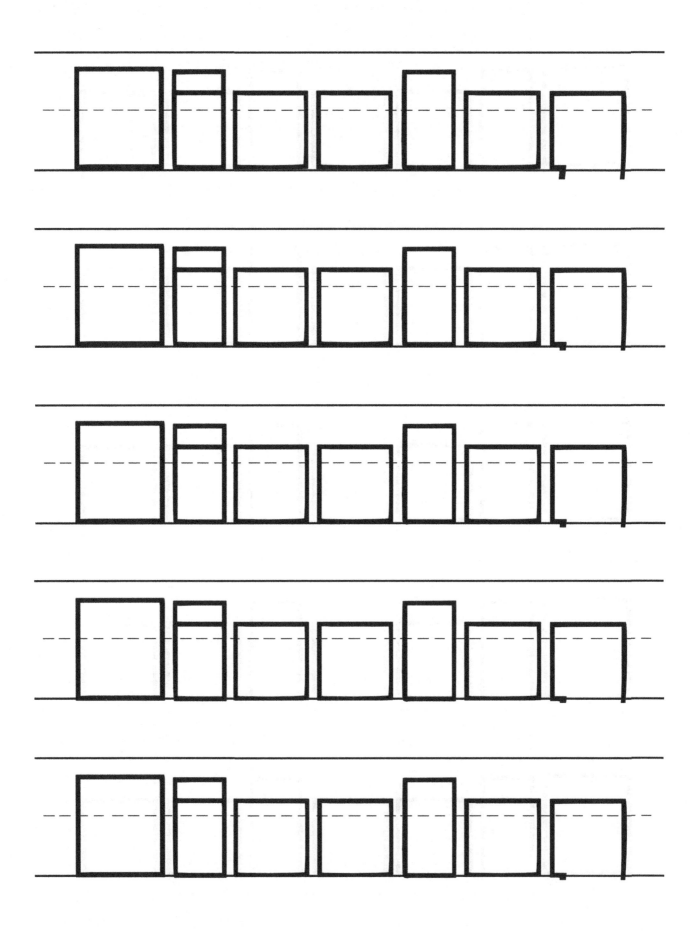

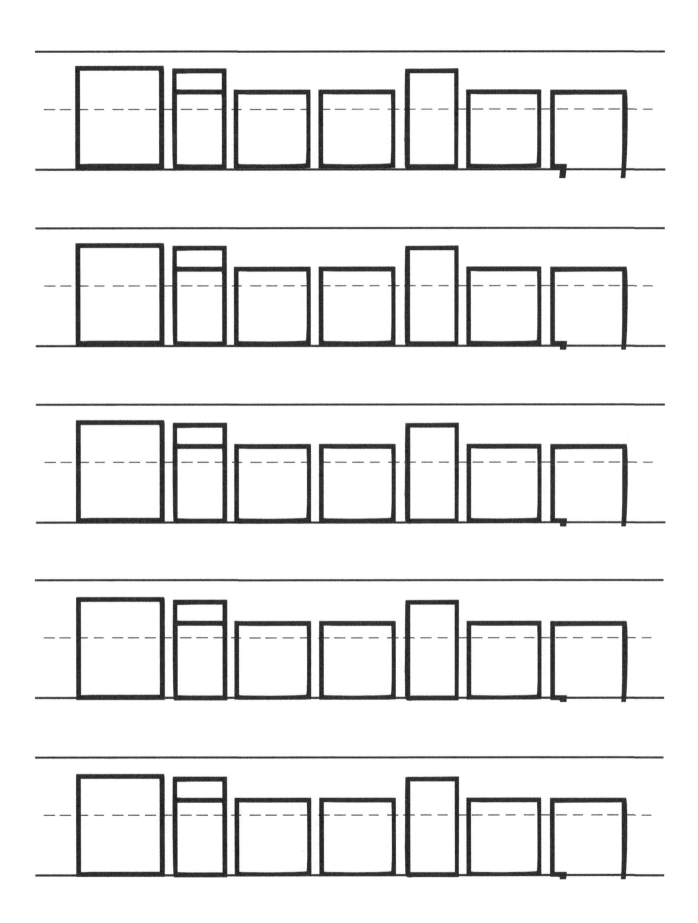

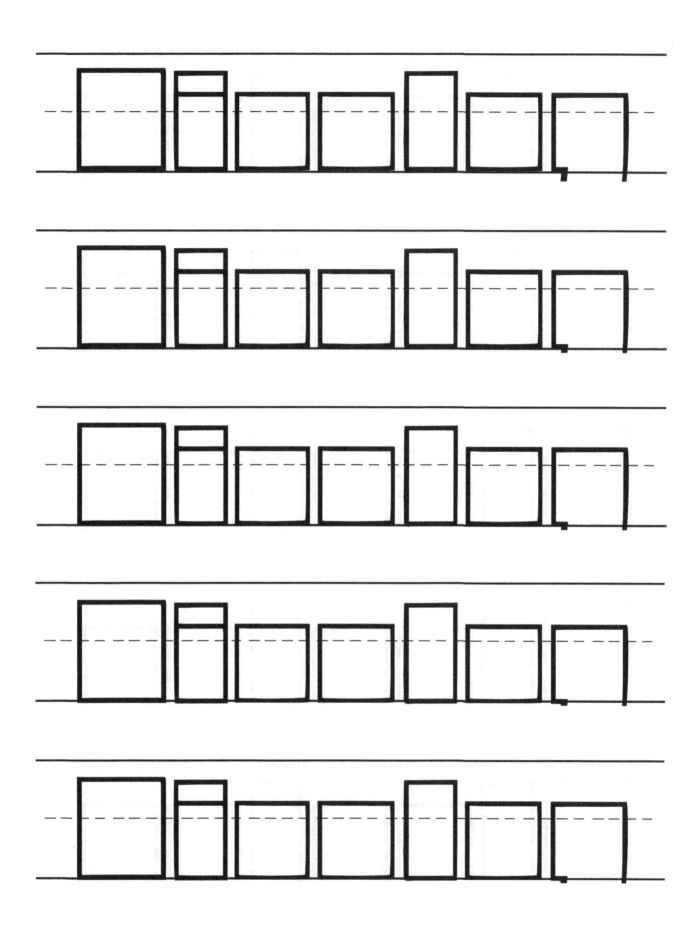

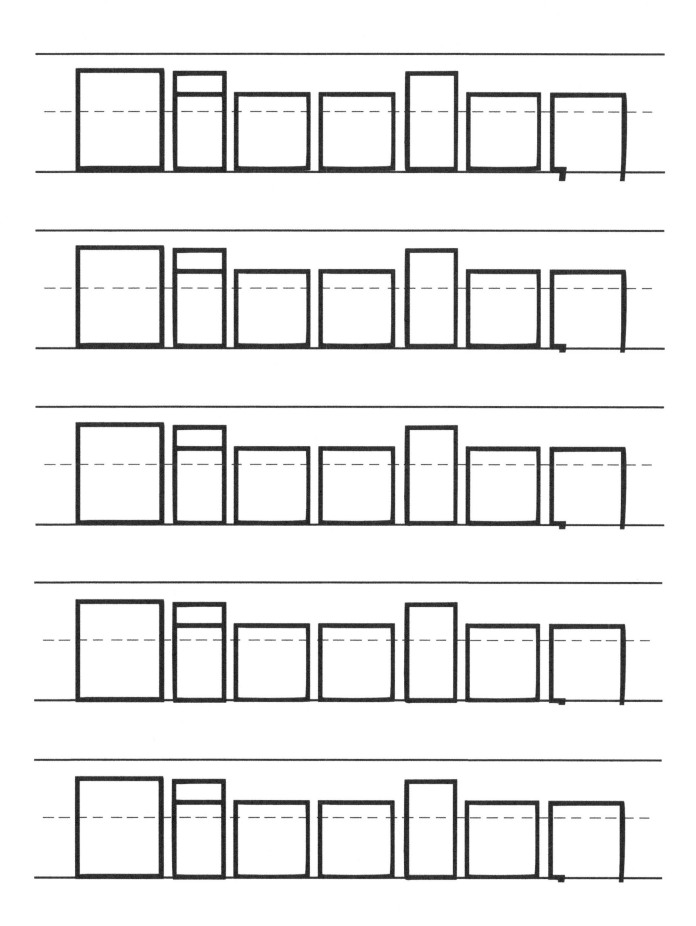

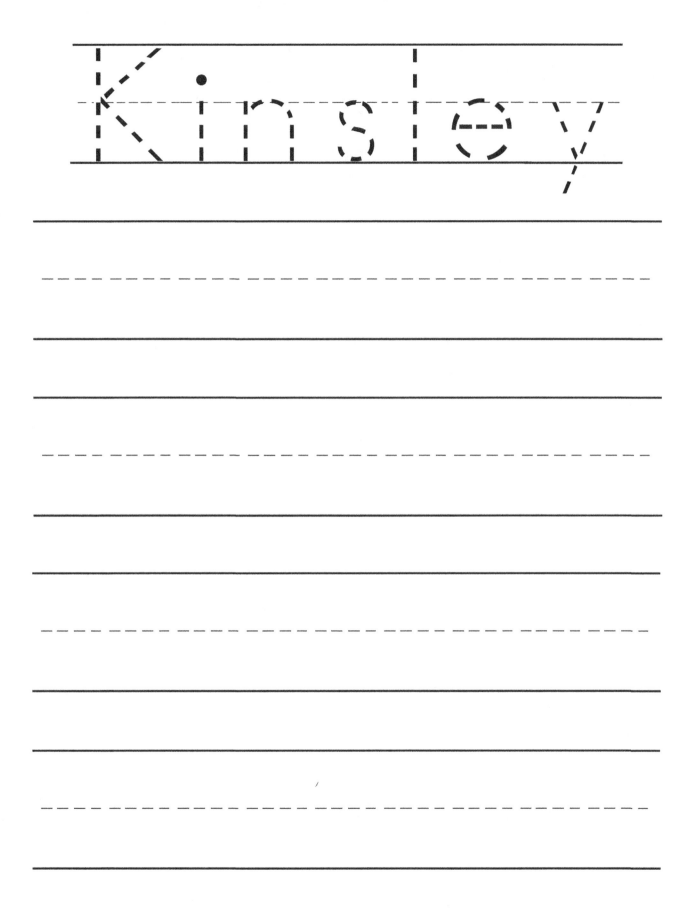

Made in United States
North Haven, CT
21 September 2023

41819104R00057

GREYSCALE

BIN TRAVELER FORM

Cut By _____ Jones _____ Qty **72** Date **06/13**

Scanned By _____ Qty _____ Date _____

Scanned Batch IDs

_____   _____   _____

Notes / Exception

_____

_____

_____

_____

_____